Embracing Duality and Cultiva...

JOURNEY
— TO —
Wholeness

VIKTORIA PIERCE

JOURNEY TO WHOLENESS WORKBOOK
Embracing Duality and Cultivating Self-Love

Book Design by
Transcendent Publishing
www.transcendentpublishing.com

Illustrations by Kira Komarianska

ISBN: 979-8-9890682-5-8

This workbook journal is a valuable tool designed to nurture your inner growth and guide your path to self-discovery. While it offers numerous benefits, it's important to keep in mind that the content provided in this workbook journal is intended for personal growth and development. This workbook is not a substitute for professional advice, therapy, or counseling, especially when you grapple with profound emotional or psychological challenges. Don't hesitate to reach out to a qualified mental health professional if you need their expertise.

This workbook is designed with your well-being in mind, aiming to be a source of positivity and self-empowerment. If, at any point, an exercise or prompt evokes discomfort or stirs negative emotions, please know that you possess the discretion to skip it or adapt it to better align with your needs.

The content within this workbook journal is protected by copyright laws. Reproduction or distribution of its contents without proper authorization is prohibited. By using this workbook journal, you acknowledge and accept these disclaimers.

It is our hope that this tool will illuminate your path, fostering a more fulfilling and purposeful life. Happy journaling, and may each page bring you closer to your innermost dreams.

Printed in the United States of America.

DEDICATION

This workbook is dedicated to the indomitable women who courageously rise above adversities and are continuously moving forward in their devoted service to life.

FREE GIFT

Embrace the opportunity to download a soul-nourishing meditation crafted to bring you a profound sense of grounding and harmonious balance as you embark on your hectic day or take on a significant project.

Take a moment to care for yourself and let it guide you to a place of inner peace and serenity.

Silent Meditation:

TABLE OF CONTENTS

"The mark of your ignorance is the depth of
your belief in injustice and tragedy.
What the caterpillar calls the end of the world,
the master calls a butterfly."

~Richard Bach,
Illusions: The Adventures of a Reluctant Messiah

This "Journey to Wholeness"
Workbook belongs to a dedicated seeker.

_____

(name)

I am ready to take the next step in my lifelong journey of exploring and growing spiritually. I am willing to delve deep into my feelings to listen to my heart's wisdom, challenge any beliefs that may hold me back, broaden my view of the world, and create a new understanding of the Universe where I feel complete and belong.

I allow myself to be honest and vulnerable in a place of self-acceptance. My heart is filled with love and respect for both myself and others.

I welcome the support of my ancestors, Guardian Angels, Celestial beings, and all beings of light during this journey. I ask for their guidance and protection and seek to learn all that I need to know today.

I feel connected to my soul's purpose and blessed as I journey toward self-discovery.

INTRODUCTION

This journal can be a companion to my book *It's Written in the Stars: Let Your Feminine Star Joyfully Shine*. Alternatively, it can be used independently as a workbook journal for those who wish to explore the notions of good and evil and right and wrong, or to restore inner balance and embrace the empowering interconnectedness of the world.

In my fictional story, Alice undergoes a transformation to become a seeker, driven to discover solutions and gain insight into her heart's desires amidst a challenging, life-altering circumstance. Along her journey, her friend Mary guides her with a worldview that embraces contrasting aspects of everything, emphasizing the need for balance while carving individual paths. Through introspection, Alice gains a fresh perspective that empowers her to find inner peace and strength, leading to significant changes in her life.

Years ago, I faced a tough, life-changing choice and turned to my mentor for guidance. She advised me to search for the best answer within my heart. She also challenged me to cultivate calmness, non-judgment, and attentiveness to my inner voice, seeking profound insights into my true soul's desires. The journey was difficult and lasted months, but the rewards were worth it.

Having this workbook journal in your hands is no coincidence; it's a sign from the Universe. It's calling you to delve into your beliefs and perceptions about yourself and others. This journey will lead you to embrace duality, rediscover your inner light, and unlock the power to achieve personal and professional success.

Inside the workbook journal, you'll discover many questions, activities, and prompts that guide you on an introspective journey. As you engage with them, your mind will gradually align with your heart's tender and caring voice. At the beginning of this process, your logical mind might feel a bit noisy and distracting, but don't worry – embrace it and wholeheartedly say "Yes!" to the transformative journey ahead.

Embrace the adventure and make the most of every moment!

Viktoria

HOW TO USE THIS WORKBOOK

STEP 1

A sincere conversation flows best when you feel safe and relaxed. Trust your intuition and choose a place that feels right for you today, to have this quiet talk with yourself. Your intuition will guide you on whether you need to arrange a sacred space with items like crystals, pictures, candles, or anything else that resonates with you. Listen to your heart and let your imagination roam freely.

STEP 2

Each passing day brings many questions, answers, challenges, and thoughts that pull us away from the present moment. Yet, our true goal lies in finding solace in the here and now. Employ any breathing technique or meditation you are familiar with to release yourself from the hustle and bustle surrounding you.

If you're unsure where to begin your journey, I invite you to try the five-minute silent meditation available on my website, viktoriapierce.com. It's a tender and compassionate way to reconnect with yourself and discover the tranquility within you.

Take a moment to check in with yourself. Feel the connection between your body, mind, and spirit. Ground yourself in the present by landing in your chair, fully experiencing the support beneath you. Listen to the rhythm of your heartbeat, and breathe in the moment.

STEP 3

Stay centered in the sense of both emptiness and fullness. Before you begin each question or prompt, take a moment to center yourself and pause.

The wonderful thing about this journal is that there are no right or wrong answers. It allows you to observe the world around you and view it from different perspectives. While journaling, try to set aside any judgmental thoughts and let your heart take the lead. Embrace the diversity of your thoughts and feelings as you journey through this journal, expressing yourself uniquely. Keep your mind calm, and let the answers come naturally from within you. When the response appears, start writing without overthinking or re-reading, even if it may not make sense (after all, who is there to judge?). Let your creativity flow naturally, and enjoy the process of creating.

Apply the same approach to the art activities as well.

In the journey toward harmony and success, remember that practice and perseverance are the keys that unlock the door of opportunities. Amidst the hustle and bustle of life, carve out precious "me" time and make a heartfelt commitment to speak to your own heart or inner child regularly, even if only for brief moments at a time. This sacred connection will nourish your soul and bring profound meaning to your path. Embrace this journey of self-discovery with love and dedication, and you'll find the beauty of transformation unfolding before you.

Your Intention and Dedication:

_____

_____

_____

_____

_____

Signature _____

Date _____

Looking Within:
Introspection and Self-Introduction

A child is born filled with pure innocence and harmony with the world. They are whole and complete in their being. However, as they grow and begin to understand the difference between good and evil, a part of their innocence fades away, and they start to lose that sense of wholeness they once had.

After years of evaluating everything (self, others, events, life, etc.) by weighing it on a scale of good and evil, the multidimensional boundless world becomes fragmented into numerous meaningless pieces. An analytical mind then organizes these fragments using judgmental values, labeling them as "good" or "bad," "right" or "wrong," according to established moral norms and ideas.

Not long ago, there was a tale on the radio about a man who possessed vast and fragrant meadows and fertile fields. One fine morning, he gathered his two grown-up sons. To the first one he said affectionately, "My dear son, I wish for you to go and gather any flowers that capture your heart and bring them to me later today." He then turned his gaze to the other. "And you, please bring me any weeds you fancy."

The sons respected their father's wishes and set out on their tasks. They diligently collected flowers and weeds throughout the day, then reunited before their father at sunset. One son presented a beautiful bouquet of wildflowers, vibrant and colorful, while the other stood before him with an armful of pleasantly scented weeds.

The father gazed upon his sons with love and spoke with a knowing smile, "At the day's end, you both collected exactly what you had looked for."

In this workbook section, you will delve into the realm of your thoughts, where the very essence of making choices, like focusing on gathering flowers and weeds, originates. Take this opportunity to explore this domain playfully, but remember to be sincere with yourself. Embrace this chance to unite the fragments of your uniqueness, completing the puzzle of your true self once more.

1. Take a moment to describe yourself and reflect on your recurring thoughts about your attributes. Start the very first sentence of your description with the words "I am ...."

2. When it comes to your physical appearance, how do you speak to yourself?

3. In thinking about your role as a friend today, how would you assess yourself?

_____

_____

_____

_____

_____

_____

_____

_____

_____

_____

4. As you reflect on your role as a daughter/son today, how would you evaluate yourself?

_____

_____

_____

_____

_____

_____

_____

_____

_____

5. As you contemplate your role as a partner/husband/wife today, how would you assess yourself?

_____

_____

_____

_____

_____

_____

_____

_____

_____

_____

6. As you ponder your role as a parent today, how would you assess yourself?

_____

_____

_____

_____

_____

_____

_____

_____

_____

_____

_____

7. As you consider your role as an employer/employee today, how would you assess yourself?

_____

_____

_____

_____

_____

_____

_____

_____

_____

8. As you reflect on your spiritual journey today, how would you evaluate yourself as a spiritual being?

_____

_____

_____

_____

_____

_____

_____

_____

_____

Considering the above responses, how would you rate yourself on a scale from 0 (awful) to 10 (perfect)?

0____1____2____3____4____5____6____7____8____9____10

If your chosen number is less than 10 (perfect), what qualities do you believe you would need to perceive yourself as excellent or good enough?

_____

_____

_____

_____

_____

_____

_____

_____

_____

_____

_____

_____

_____

_____

We often scrutinize our worth through the lens of others – parents, teachers, classmates, and those around us. Their judgments are shaped by their own life experiences, beliefs, and moral values, and a limited scale of good and evil that might not fully grasp the depths of our true essence.

Yet, with unwavering certainty, we realize that our worth extends beyond these external viewpoints. We are unique intricate beings, yearning to grasp our authentic selves beyond mere subjective comments.

In writing about yourself, whose unspoken voice serves you as the primary judge?

(Hint: The initial image or thought that comes to mind is an accurate response.)

Prompt of the Day: How Courage Fuels Self-Exploration

Unfolding the Self:
Introspection and Unveiling through Expansion

Frequently, we admire the achievements of others but overlook our skills and talents. Now, it's time to shine and claim your place on the walk of fame in your life. This workbook section is designed to broaden your self-perception to boost your self-esteem.

1. Take a moment to jot down ALL the personal skills and talents you have acquired and cultivated up until now.

My Skills & Talents

_____

_____

_____

_____

_____

_____

_____

_____

_____

_____

_____

_____

_____

_____

Continue adding to this list even after you have completed all the activities in this workbook.

2. Describe the unique experience you went through.

_____

_____

_____

_____

_____

_____

_____

_____

_____

_____

_____

_____

_____

_____

_____

_____

_____

_____

_____

_____

_____

Persist in enhancing this list even after you finish all the activities in this workbook.

3. I'm grateful to myself for...

_____

_____

_____

_____

_____

_____

_____

_____

_____

_____

Persist in expanding this list even after you have finished all the activities in this workbook.

A Tapestry of Success: Your Personal Collage

Harness the power of your creative imagination to craft a collage that represents your success. For this activity, choose images that genuinely speak to your soul, reflecting the moments of triumph and victory in your life's journey. Place these pictures on the next page, or gently transfer them onto your canvas or board. As you do so, allow your heart to guide you, immersing yourself in the emotions that surface during this intimate process. Let the energy of gratitude and joy fill your heart as you weave together a beautiful tapestry of your accomplishments, a collage that captures the essence of your unique path.

As each image finds its perfect place, and you feel delighted in the arrangement, secure your collage pieces with glue and allow your masterpiece to dry. May this artwork remind you of your remarkable path, filling you with pride and inspiration for the journey ahead.

Add your collage here...

Looking Within:
A Glimpse Through the Mirror

In this profound journey, you are invited to explore a different dimension beyond the confines of a mirror. Picture yourself through the eyes of celestial beings or the ever-watchful gaze of your Guardian Angels. Embrace this tender reflection with an open heart, letting go of doubts or inner debates. Trust in the wisdom that arises from this heartfelt exploration as you unveil profound insights and perspectives about yourself. Let this sacred experience remind you of the Divine love and support surrounding you, guiding you through self-discovery and growth.

1. View yourself through the eyes of beings of light and express your qualities from their perspective. Start the very first sentence of your description with the words "[Your name] is ...."

_____

_____

_____

_____

_____

_____

_____

2. From the perspective of beings of light, how would they describe your appearance?

_____

_____

_____

_____

_____

_____

_____

3. Imagine yourself as a friend, viewed through the eyes of beings of light, and describe the qualities and essence they see in you.

_____

_____

_____

_____

_____

_____

4. Imagine yourself as a daughter/son, viewed through the eyes of beings of light, and describe the qualities and essence they see in you.

_____

_____

_____

_____

_____

_____

5. With the gaze of beings of light upon you, describe yourself today as a partner/ wife/husband, expressing the qualities and attributes they perceive in your role.

_____

_____

_____

_____

_____

_____

6. Imagine yourself as a parent, viewed through the eyes of beings of light, and describe the qualities and essence they see in you.

_____

_____

_____

_____

_____

_____

_____

7. From the vantage point of beings of light, evaluate yourself today as an employer or an employee, considering the qualities and perspectives they observe in these roles.

_____

_____

_____

_____

_____

_____

_____

8. In the tender embrace of beings of light, how would they characterize you as a spiritual being?

_____

_____

_____

_____

_____

Considering your responses above, how would you assess yourself on a scale from 0 (awful) to 10 (perfect)?

0____1____2____3____4____5____6____7____8____9____10

Where does the essence of your life energy flow today as you reflect on your self-evaluation? Does it gravitate toward collecting flowers, embracing the positive aspects of your being, or does it lean toward gathering weeds, where you may focus on the challenges and negatives? Embrace this contemplation with gentle introspection, for it holds the key to understanding the direction of your heart and soul.

_____

_____

_____

_____

_____

_____

_____

_____

_____

_____

_____

_____

_____

_____

_____

_____

_____

_____

Prompt of the Day: Distinguishing Flowers from Weeds

The story of gathering flowers and weeds sparks a deeper inquiry: What distinguishes one from the other?

Reflecting on Relationships: The Bond with Parents

In the sacred moment, we step into the realm of existence, embracing this wondrous reality we call life on the beautiful planet Earth; we find ourselves entwined in the delicate dance of relationships with all that surrounds us. No one stands alone on this earthly canvas of life; we are interconnected, interdependent threads woven intricately. The interplay of our experiences shapes us, molds us, and guides us toward growth and understanding.

Our actions and emotions ripple outward, affecting the lives of those we touch, while their presence leaves an indelible mark upon our souls.

The inaugural encounter in the realm of relationships unfolds with our mothers. This first experience holds the potential to leave an indelible mark, shaping our future connections with partners, children, and others in profound ways.

1. Compose a sincere letter addressed to your mother.

Allow yourself the freedom of time for this writing; it may span over several days or even weeks. There's no pressure to send the letter to your mom or read it to her unless you feel compelled to do so. This heartfelt letter serves as a means to rekindle a profound connection with the source of life as you reestablish your bond with your mother, a vessel who received life from her parents and passed it on to you. Embrace this process with gentleness and reverence, as it opens the gate to the precious gift of life you have inherited.

Amid this journey, treat yourself with tenderness and kindness, embracing each step with a gentle heart.

A Letter to My Mother

_____

_____

_____

_____

_____

_____

_____

_____

_____

_____

_____

_____

_____

_____

_____

_____

_____

_____

_____

Truly yours,

(Your name)

2. Compose a sincere letter addressed to your father.

As we grow, we embark on a journey of exploration in the world around us, and our father becomes the guiding companion on this adventure.

Just as he served as a vessel, passing the gift of life to you, he plays a pivotal role in shaping your path.

This writing can take several days or weeks to complete. Embrace the freedom of time as you pour your thoughts and feelings onto paper. Remember, there's no obligation to send the letter to your dad or read it to him unless your heart desires it.

This letter serves as a powerful tool to reestablish a connection with the source of life, empowering you on your journey. Delve into the essence of your origins to unlock the strength and wisdom passed down through generations. Embrace this process with love and authenticity, for it holds the key to a deeper understanding of yourself.

As you embark on this journey, remember to be gentle and compassionate with yourself.

A Letter to My Father

Truly yours,

(Your name)

7-Day Quest:
Unraveling the Universe's Whispers to You

Throughout the day, we encounter various individuals, animals, plants, and more. Engaging in different events and situations, we tend to respond automatically, influenced by our ingrained habits, beliefs, attitudes, and other factors.

These reflections, spanning 7 days, present a new and invigorating outlook on the individuals you've interacted with and the circumstances you've encountered. Their primary goal is to sharpen your mindfulness in the present moment, enabling you to recognize potential solutions amid challenges and empowering you to make well-informed decisions when confronted with obstacles.

In my book, *It's Written in the Stars,* the heroine says, "We should embrace those who challenge us, for they provide us with an opportunity to evolve and grow." Now, let's examine if her perspective holds true.

Day 1. Compile a list of individuals you encountered today and assess the emotions each elicited in you.

Today, _____, 20___, the Universe talked to me through the following people:

Person I met today	Good because	Bad because

A lesson I learned from a good person is... (Share the lesson you learned or received from this person's influence or actions.)

_____

_____

_____

_____

_____

_____

_____

This lesson makes me more robust/better/wiser.

- True
- False

The outcome of this lesson is

- God
- Bad

A lesson I learned from an evil person is... (Share the lesson you learned or received from this person's influence or actions.)

_____

_____

_____

_____

_____

_____

_____

This lesson makes me stronger/better/wiser.

- True
- False

The outcome of this lesson is

- Good
- Bad

Day 2. Compile a list of individuals you encountered today and assess the emotions each elicited in you.

Today, _____, 20___, the Universe talk to me through the following people…

Person I met today	Good because	Bad because

A lesson I learned from a good person is… (Share the lesson you learned or received from this person's influence or actions.)

_____

_____

_____

_____

_____

_____

This lesson makes me more robust/better/wiser.

- True
- False

The outcome of this lesson is

- God
- Bad

A lesson I learned from an evil person is… (Share the lesson you learned or received from this person's influence or actions.)

_____

_____

_____

_____

_____

_____

_____

_____

_____

_____

_____

_____

This lesson makes me stronger/better/wiser.

- True
- False

The outcome of this lesson is

- Good
- Bad

Day 3. Compile a list of individuals you encountered today and assess the emotions each elicited in you.

Today, _____, 20___, the Universe talk to me through the following people…

Person I met today	Good because	Bad because

A lesson I learned from a good person is… (Share the lesson you learned or received from this person's influence or actions.)

_____

_____

_____

_____

_____

_____

_____

_____

_____

_____

_____

This lesson makes me more robust/better/wiser.

- True
- False

The outcome of this lesson is

- God
- Bad

A lesson I learned from an evil person is… (Share the lesson you learned or received from this person's influence or actions.)

This lesson makes me stronger/better/wiser.

- True
- False

The outcome of this lesson is

- Good
- Bad

Day 4. Compile a list of individuals you encountered today and assess the emotions each elicited in you.

Today, _____, 20___, the Universe talk to me through the following people…

Person I met today	Good because	Bad because

A lesson I learned from a good person is… (Share the lesson you learned or received from this person's influence or actions.)

_____

_____

_____

_____

_____

_____

_____

_____

_____

_____

_____

This lesson makes me more robust/better/wiser.

- True
- False

The outcome of this lesson is

- God
- Bad

A lesson I learned from an evil person is… (Share the lesson you learned or received from this person's influence or actions.)

_____

_____

_____

_____

_____

_____

_____

_____

_____

_____

_____

This lesson makes me stronger/better/wiser.

- True
- False

The outcome of this lesson is

- Good
- Bad

Day 5. Compile a list of individuals you encountered today and assess the emotions each elicited in you.

Today, _____, 20___, the Universe talk to me through the following people…

Person I met today	Good because	Bad because

A lesson I learned from a good person is… (Share the lesson you learned or received from this person's influence or actions.)

_____

_____

_____

_____

_____

_____

_____

_____

_____

_____

_____

_____

_____

This lesson makes me more robust/better/wiser.

- True
- False

The outcome of this lesson is

- God
- Bad

A lesson I learned from an evil person is… (Share the lesson you learned or received from this person's influence or actions.)

_____

_____

_____

_____

_____

_____

_____

_____

_____

_____

_____

_____

This lesson makes me stronger/better/wiser.

- True
- False

The outcome of this lesson is

- Good
- Bad

Day 6. Compile a list of individuals you encountered today and assess the emotions each elicited in you.

Today, _____, 20___, the Universe talk to me through the following people…

Person I met today	Good because	Bad because

A lesson I learned from a good person is… (Share the lesson you learned or received from this person's influence or actions.)

_____

_____

_____

_____

_____

_____

_____

_____

_____

_____

_____

_____

This lesson makes me more robust/better/wiser.

- True
- False

The outcome of this lesson is

- God
- Bad

A lesson I learned from an evil person is… (Share the lesson you learned or received from this person's influence or actions.)

_____

_____

_____

_____

_____

_____

_____

_____

_____

_____

This lesson makes me stronger/better/wiser.

- True
- False

The outcome of this lesson is

- Good
- Bad

Day 7. Compile a list of individuals you encountered today and assess the emotions each elicited in you.

Today, _____, 20___, the Universe talk to me through the following people...

Person I met today	Good because	Bad because

A lesson I learned from a good person is... (Share the lesson you learned or received from this person's influence or actions.)

_____

_____

_____

_____

_____

_____

_____

_____

_____

_____

_____

_____

This lesson makes me more robust/better/wiser.

- True
- False

The outcome of this lesson is

- God
- Bad

A lesson I learned from an evil person is… (Share the lesson you learned or received from this person's influence or actions.)

_____

_____

_____

_____

_____

_____

_____

_____

_____

_____

_____

This lesson makes me stronger/better/wiser.

- True
- False

The outcome of this lesson is

- Good
- Bad

Synthesize your thoughts and emotions, then craft a concluding statement encapsulating your overall perspective or findings.

Prompt of the Day. Change: A Journey Through Both the Light and the Shadows

A change is good because ...

A change is awful because ...

Life's Reflections:
Embracing the Good and Learning from the Bad

In the profound moment when our ancestors tasted the fruit from the Tree of Knowledge, their entire perception of the world underwent a transformative shift. It was like a veil had been lifted, revealing a new reality of contrasting emotions and values. The once harmonious and seamless existence was now defined by dichotomies: sin and innocence, good and evil, just and unjust. Such a pivotal moment in history echoes the complexities of human existence and reminds us of the profound depth and challenges that life bestows upon us.

Within this workbook section, you will embark on a journey to delve into the profound contrast between good and evil, drawing upon real-life examples from your own experiences. As you explore these concepts, you will gain insight into how they intricately intertwine and influence the larger tapestry of the world.

Create a list of the most remarkable events you have been a part of recently, along with a heartfelt expression of your emotions towards each of them.

Last week/month/year, I was involved in the following events…

GOOD EVENTS	BAD EVENTS

Please select the most uplifting and positive event from your list and provide a detailed description of it, relishing its brightness and significance.

The event is good because ...

_____

_____

_____

_____

_____

_____

_____

_____

Reflect upon the positive event you experienced and share the valuable lesson you learned.

_____

_____

_____

_____

_____

_____

_____

_____

_____

_____

This lesson makes me more robust/better/wiser.

- True
- False

Notes:

_____

_____

_____

_____

_____

_____

_____

_____

_____

Please choose the most impactful and challenging adverse event from your list, and provide a comprehensive description, delving into its details and implications.

The event is bad because…

_____

_____

_____

_____

_____

_____

_____

_____

_____

_____

Share the lesson you learned from the problematic or adverse event, highlighting the insights and wisdom gained through navigating its challenges.

_____

_____

_____

_____

_____

_____

_____

_____

This lesson makes me more robust/better/wiser.

- True
- False

This day brought more good events than bad.

- True
- False

Notes:

_____

_____

_____

_____

_____

_____

_____

Looking Within: Draw a Cosmic Self

In my book, the heroine received numerous gifts from celestial beings, ranging from creative expression and courage to intuition and transformation. Each blessing bestowed by Mercury, Mars, Venus, Jupiter, Saturn, Neptune, Pluto, Sun, Uranus, and Earth contributed to her unique cosmic portrait and guided her on a profound journey of self-discovery.

1. Dive deep into the cherished gift bestowed upon you by celestial beings that holds the utmost significance and appreciation in your heart, and express its profound impact on your life.

   I am grateful for the gift of …

   _____

   _____

   _____

   _____

   _____

   _____

   _____

   _____

   _____

   _____

   _____

2. Reflect on the celestial bodies that welcomed you into this world, and create your cosmic self-portrait with pencils or paint to honor the unique gifts from each planet. Embrace these enchanting connections to the stars, igniting a heartfelt exploration of your distinct qualities. This cosmic journey of self-discovery holds the essence of your soul's path and the celestial blessings that shaped your journey.

Draw your cosmic self-portrait here...

Looking Within:
Unveiling the Inner Child Through Self-Reflection

At times, a profound ache reminds us that a part of ourselves longs for love and attention, mainly when our inner child didn't receive enough parental affection in the past. Now is the moment to acknowledge that our parents' role in bringing us into this world has fulfilled its purpose, and we must recognize that our life belongs solely to us. Let us embrace our life with gratitude and the responsibility of caring for our inner child who may be trapped in the past, yearning for our loving care and nurturing.

This journey of self-reflection serves as a powerful means to reconnect with your inner child, allowing it to flourish and evolve into a place of growth and maturity.

1. Write a letter to little yourself.

Compose a heartfelt letter to the cherished inner child within you, embracing your past self with love, compassion, and understanding. In this letter of boundless love, assure your inner child that there are no time limitations for your meetings, and promise to come together to offer unwavering support, care, and nourishment regularly.

Letter to My Inner Child

_____

_____

_____

_____

_____

_____

_____

_____

_____

_____

_____

_____

_____

_____

_____

_____

_____

_____

_____

_____

_____

With all my love,

(Your name)

2. Draw your inner child.

Imagine and connect with your inner child, envisioning the essence of your younger self filled with innocence, curiosity, and boundless imagination.

3. Write a letter from your inner child to yourself.

Long ago, there were moments when others would inquire, "Whom do you aspire to become?" This question, at times, vexed and bewildered you. The road ahead was shrouded in uncertainty and haze. Revisit the memories of your childhood self and compose a heartfelt letter from your inner child to the adult version of yourself, expressing their feelings, hopes, and desires and offering insights and reminders that resonate from the innocence and wisdom of their perspective.

An Epistle to My Grown Self

With all the love and warmth of a child's heart,

Your Inner Child

Self-Reflection: 7-Day Self-Care Challenge

Every passing day, we are confronted with an overwhelming array of choices and decisions. Each choice carries an unseen burden as we weigh it against an invisible scale of what is deemed "right" or "wrong." This innate desire to belong to a community and family drives us to seek approval and validation, hoping to be seen as good and virtuous in their eyes. Yet, in this pursuit, we may compromise our true selves, betraying our authentic selves. There is no judgment here; it is simply the reality of human nature.

This section of the workbook serves to raise your awareness of situations in which saying yes to someone else may inadvertently lead to denying your own needs and telling yourself no.

In the upcoming week, your objective is to observe your thoughts, feelings, and actions closely. Take non-judgmental notes on any occasions where you may have unintentionally disregarded your true self or, conversely, prioritized your heartfelt desires.

Day 1. Today,_____,20___, I betrayed myself when...

_____

_____

_____

_____

_____

_____

_____

_____

_____

_____

_____

I prioritized self-care and remained steadfast when…

The lesson I have taken away from this is...

Day 2. Today,_____,20___, I betrayed myself when...

_____

_____

_____

_____

_____

_____

_____

_____

_____

_____

_____

I prioritized self-care and remained steadfast when...

_____

_____

_____

_____

_____

_____

_____

_____

_____

_____

_____

_____

The lesson I have taken away from this is...

_____

_____

_____

_____

_____

_____

_____

_____

_____

_____

Day 3. Today,_____,20___, I betrayed myself when...

_____

_____

_____

_____

_____

_____

_____

_____

_____

_____

I prioritized self-care and remained steadfast when…

The lesson I have taken away from this is...

Day 4. Today,_____,20___, I betrayed myself when...

I prioritized self-care and remained steadfast when...

The lesson I have taken away from this is...

_____

_____

_____

_____

_____

_____

_____

_____

_____

_____

Day 5. Today,_____,20___, I betrayed myself when...

_____

_____

_____

_____

_____

_____

_____

_____

_____

I prioritized self-care and remained steadfast when…

The lesson I have taken away from this is...

Day 6. Today,_____,20___, I betrayed myself when...

I prioritized self-care and remained steadfast when...

The lesson I have taken away from this is...

_____

_____

_____

_____

_____

_____

_____

_____

_____

_____

Day 7. Today,_____,20___, I betrayed myself when...

_____

_____

_____

_____

_____

_____

_____

_____

I prioritized self-care and remained steadfast when…

The lesson I have taken away from this is...

Combine your thoughts and emotions to create a synthesis, and then write a concluding statement summarizing your overall perspective or findings.

_____

_____

_____

_____

_____

_____

_____

_____

_____

_____

_____

_____

_____

_____

_____

_____

_____

_____

_____

_____

_____

_____

_____

_____

Create a collage with the theme "I am loved. I belong. I am enough."

Unleash your creative imagination and select various pictures or images representing what you envision for your joyful life. Aim to include pictures that fulfill all spheres of your life, such as personal, social, cultural, and more. Let your collage be a reflection of your dreams and aspirations.

Arrange the chosen images on the next page or transfer them to your canvas or board. As you do so, pay close attention to your emotions and feelings while finding the desired images. Remember, your wishes hold the potential to come true, so ensure that you genuinely want and need each picture you place. Let your intuition guide you as you find the perfect places for each image in your collage.

Once each image has found its perfect place and you are delighted with the final arrangement, carefully glue your collage pieces in position. Allow your masterpiece to dry, and then take a moment to savor the accomplishment. Enjoy the beautiful creation you have brought to life!

Add your collage here...

Prompt of the Day. How Being True to Yourself and Others Can Transform Lives

LET YOUR STAR SHINE!

Congratulations on achieving one of the many milestones along your journey of self-exploration and personal growth!

Now that you have absorbed all you've learned and drawn your conclusions take this opportunity to re-evaluate yourself.

On a scale from 0 (awful) to 10 (perfect), how do you perceive the value of your unique self?

0____1____2____3____4____5____6____7____8____9____10

If you selected any number less than 10 (perfect) and would like to continue this journey to wholeness in search of inner harmony, forgiveness, and reconciliation through expended perception and spiritual growth, below are ways I may assist you.

- Visit viktoriapierce.com to schedule a one-on-one session.
- Follow my Family Constellations Center Facebook page for the Family Constellations workshop and the Universal Orders class schedule: facebook.com/pierce.familyconstellations
- Watch my YouTube channel to learn more about Family Constellations and Family Constellators: youtube.com/@viktoriapierce4690/videos

As the pages of this workbook gently close, let your journey of self-discovery persist, embracing the role of an observer in the ebb and flow of days, always cherishing the invaluable gift of your uniqueness and the breathtaking beauty that dwells within you.

ABOUT THE AUTHOR

Viktoria's life journey has been a captivating odyssey, spanning from the heart of Soviet Ukraine to the vibrant shores of the Gulf Coast in Texas. Raised in Kyiv, she grew up amidst the contrasting worlds of her father's construction work and her mother's melodious opera performances. Driven by an unquenchable thirst for knowledge, she pursued a Master's in Economics and Information Control Systems and Technologies, laying the groundwork for her future endeavors.

Viktoria's professional path has been diverse, starting as a humble baker and steadily climbing the ladder to become a successful banker and esteemed general manager in the outsourcing industry. However, her life took a transformative turn when her adventurous spirit led her to explore distant lands like the Czech Republic, the UK, Turkey, and more. It was a profound journey to India at the turn of the millennium that reshaped her entire trajectory. This pivotal experience gave her the courage to leave behind her past life, including her marriage, and embark on a fresh start in the United States with her two youngest children.

Her unyielding faith in unseen forces guiding her life's course encouraged her to seize opportunities in her new homeland. Determined to overcome language barriers, she mastered English and began teaching economics at a local college. Yet, it was her long-cherished dream of studying Family Constellation work, inspired by Bert Hellinger, that eventually materialized in 2013. Through intensive training in Germany and Mexico, she became a certified Family Constellations facilitator, expanding her consciousness and honing her skills as an educator.

Empowered by her transformative training, Viktoria is devoted to bringing positive change into people's lives. She helps individuals forge a strong sense of self, meaningful relationships, and a harmonious balance between their personal and professional spheres. When she's not guiding others on their journeys, Viktoria finds solace and inspiration in her cherished garden, where she learns from nature's wisdom, unveiling profound interconnections between the visible and the invisible.

Today, Viktoria resides and works along the picturesque Gulf Coast of Texas, extending her reach through online sessions and Family Constellations workshops both locally and internationally. With a heart brimming with compassion and a wealth of knowledge, she remains steadfast in her mission to empower individuals in their pursuit of fulfillment and harmony.

Notes:

Milton Keynes UK
Ingram Content Group UK Ltd.
UKHW050149020124
435290UK00004B/14